# LOUDERSHIP

✦✦✦

Eric Geary

PAVILION BOOKS
PO Box 8653
Lexington, KY 40533

*Pavilion* books

Visit the Author's website at www.loudership.com

Printed in the United States of America
ISBN 978-0-9827519-85

Cover Design: Andy Coleman
Interior Design: Rhonda Dragomir

# ENDORSEMENTS

‡ ‡ ‡

I DON'T READ MANY LEADERSHIP BOOKS because I don't need to and because it takes away from my time on the open sea. But LOUDERSHIP...INCREDIBLE... truly....INCREDIBLE.  Mark my words and my ellipsis's, this guy has climbed the summit of leadership and is looking down on the rest of us.

*Phil Hybels*

I'M A LEADERSHIP GURU, seriously. I've written books, penned articles, led conferences and consulted some of the greatest leaders you've never heard of. I have honestly never heard such revolutionary principles as you will find in LOUDERSHIP. And that my friends, is not even close to refutable.

*Juan Maxwell*

I'M RE-THINKING EVERYTHING I've ever read or written on leadership. The content in this book will rock your leadership world. Seriously, He's good people, real good. I promise. None better. I don't really even know where I've been pointing for all these years anymore. This guy is true north.

*Antony Stanley*

# DEDICATION

I dedicate this book to three extremely important people: Me, myself, and I.

Oh, and a shout out to my bootstraps.

# Contents

# INTRODUCTION

—— ✦✦✦ ——

INTRODUCTIONS ARE USUALLY JUST FUZZY WORDS, trying to convince you that the rest of what they say is going to be brilliant.

You can TRUST me, I'm brilliant. So, I won't waste your time or mine.

I've read all the "Leadership" books. Well, most of them. Okay, a few. I've also been to a ton of leadership conferences. Quite honestly, I can't stand any more of this nonsense. I've been holding my tongue for far too long. So, it's time to increase the volume of my own opinion and share my views on leadership with the world.

It's a new paradigm of leadership...nah...scratch that...it's a LEADERSHIP REVOLUTION! **BOOM!**

I call it LOUDERSHIP. Yep—I said it—I am a LOUDER not a leader. There are many of us out there calling ourselves leaders but in reality we are one step above the leader. We know it, others know it. We're different. We stand out.  I am just the first one bold enough to make the proclamation and capture the principles we LOUDERS use on paper.

So this book is step one in releasing the revolution. In these pages, I highlight leadership principles that you and I have been taught for years and then—BLOW them away—**BOOM!**

Then I swoop in with a LOUDERSHIP principle. It's good stuff. In fact, its NEXT LEVEL stuff and I promise that these strategies will AMPLIFY your leadership.

Are you ready for LOUDERSHIP? **BOOM!**

# INTRODUCTION 2

YEAH, I KNOW IT'S UNUSUAL to have two introductions to a book. **BOOM!**

But quite honestly, I've never written a book and I had a little more to say but couldn't figure out a good transition after I asked the "Are you ready" question. It was just so poignant that I felt like I would diminish the power of it by putting some more words after it.

Plus, this part is just kind of housekeeping really. You need to know some stuff before you go on.
1) I like hyphens and ALL CAPS.
2) I don't really edit stuff. Editing takes time. Time is money.
3) Your concern with grammar, punctuation and spelling is no concern of mine.
4) Some of my chapters are really, *really* short. That's because more words weren't necessary or I couldn't think of more words.

5) This book is TOTALLY satire. Don't be offended.

# 1
# THERE'S NO "I"
# IN TEAM-

## BUT THERE IS AN "M" AND AN "E"

———— ✦✦✦ ————

YOU'VE UNDOUBTEDLY HEARD IT SAID, from some leader—somewhere, that "There is no I in team." It's quippy sure, and alphabetically accurate but it doesn't take into account that there is an M and an E in the word TEAM.

See that, I BLEW IT UP. That's how I do it.
**BOOM!**

The Leadership Principle being taught by the gurus when they say that there "Is no I in TEAM" is sometimes referred to as "Servant Leadership." I've heard it has occasionally produced some astounding results. I can tell you this though—it's NEVER worked for ME. I've tried it, on several occasions. Okay, I tried it once. Uh.....DISASTER!

I say Servant Leadership has run its course.

The LOUDERSHIP principle that I employ is the opposite of Servant Leadership. While I must agree that alphabetically there is no I in team, there is an M and an E. The M and the E are actually the most important letters in the word TEAM. Take away the M and the E and what is left? Not much I say, just an "A" and a "T." All you can spell with those two letters are "AT" and "TA." Both of those are lame words.

But the M and the E...you put those together and you have something.

The ME is the most important part of the team. It's not even arguable really. Don't believe me, check the Org Chart. That's ME up there at the top. Those people under my name are the rest of the TEAM. If they were the most important, they would be at the top. But they're not are they? They're under ME, in small rectangular boxes strangely shaped like stepping stones.

A Servant Leader flips the chart upside down and sees their role as empowering and equipping the TEAM.

That's NOT, I repeat NOT a good idea.

The bottom line is that I worked remotely hard to get to that spot. This little box is my box and this chart will not be flipped upside down so that the rest of the people around me will feel valued.

In fact, I resent the idea that flipping a chart upside down would even make a change in MY organization. LOUDERSHIP always rises to the top. You can draw the chart in concentric circles and have an "organic" structure if you want, but at the end of the day, my little circle floats to the top. It's just that way.

I have more to say on this topic but I decided not to.

# 2
# HIRE DULL

———— ✦✦✦ ————

THE GURUS TELL US TO HIRE THE BEST and the brightest people we can find and put them on your team. Let me blow this one up. It is NOT a good plan.

As the LOUDER, I say hire DULL. **BOOM!**

You can't possibly argue with this logic. If my ultimate goal is to stay on the top box, why in the WORLD would I put smarter people around me? How can I outshine all them smart people?

I can't. That's why I hire dull.

Imagine the situation you put yourself in as a leader if your board of directors or deacons or governing authority of any form looks down the line and sees a bunch of talent. It's natural for them to start thinking about the future of your organization. How things might be in good hands when a transition is needed. Don't put them in that kind of a predicament. It's not even right for you to assume that the board has a clue about the future of YOUR organization.

LOUDERS hold power, prestige and position. Hiring smart people is the WORST thing you can do. Before you know it, one of these cats is going to do something that makes them look good. If they look good, it makes you look less good.

What if one of these people actually wants your job? All (both) of the leadership books (magazine articles) I read talk about succession as if it is a good thing for a leader to be training up the next leader. Uh, NO, it's not good. It's dumb. In fact, it's real dumb.

I heard a guy one time tell me that success without succession is failure. Uh...that doesn't make a lick of sense to me. Success is success...slice it, dice it, throw it in a pan and let it simmer. Boil it, bake it, and deep fry it if you want...but it is...what it is... and it is...success. To say otherwise refutes every law of the English language and most of the Canadian language too. The LOUDER doesn't think or talk about succession or sustainability. It weakens your position. The last thing I want anyone to see, as the LOUDER, is weakness. Vulnerability is not becoming. The leaders say that authenticity and vulnerability are good for team dynamics. They say it creates a culture of trust among the team.

But remember, as a LOUDER, the team is unimportant.

See the attached Org Chart if you need a reminder, dullard.

# 3
# THINK INSIDE THE BOX

—— ✦✦✦ ——

YEP, I SAID IT. Think INSIDE the box.

Do you know how many times I've heard "Think Outside the Box"at leadership conferences? At least 4200 times. It's old. It's outdated.

That's why I blow it up...

Think INSIDE the Box.

The LOUDER strikes again. **BOOM!**

Do any of you know when and where the term "Think outside the Box" originated? It originated from a 9 dot exercise management consultants used in the 70's and 80's to challenge people to think from a different perspective. To complete the exercise, you had to connect the 9 dots with three moves of your pencil without lifting the pencil off the paper. Let's all give Kudos to some smart guy for thinking this one up.

Since then, almost every leader I know has used the phrase, "Think Outside the Box" as some cute little axiom that encourages creativity and novel thinking.

But let's do some math. If we have been thinking outside the box since 1970…then where are all the good ideas now? **BOOM!**

They're *inside* the box.

Not all of them, but at least 81% of all good ideas are lying around inside that box. It's hard to argue with LOUDER logic.

Now think about the box. Picture it. It has four sides. It's brown and has a lid. It's cozy and safe. Those features are important, because if you are a LOUDER, there will come a point at which you will need to hide in there.

Prove my point? I thought so.

# 4
# VISIONATOR

——— ✦✦✦ ———

I'VE HEARD A TON of teaching at leadership conferences on "Casting Vision" or "Visioneering." Quite honestly, I don't know what either of those things mean really. It's not even in my LOUDER vocabulary. I don't really have the need to share my vision and I certainly don't have any desire to hear other people's vision.

I am actually a VISIONATOR. Yep, I destroy vision. I BLOW IT UP! It's what I do. It's LOUDERSHIP BABY! **BOOM!**

It's like I'm the Arnold Schwarzenegger of vision. I will terminate it…quickly!

In fact, I am even anti-creativity.

We have all been taught to engage and encourage creative thinking and vision. One way you can do this is to allow for open communication and brainstorming in planning meetings. But remember, you do it at your own peril.

Let's say you made a little oopsie and didn't hire dull. You actually hired some smart people with ideas. You know the ones, the kind of people that think "Outside the Box," (see chapter 5 or 3, I can't remember, I blow that one up too). These folks are on the other side of annoying. I come with the ideas and they are trying to improve them? It's usually the young ones, the bright eyed kids, fresh out of college, trying to climb the ladder and take you down.

The LOUDERSHIP principle is simple— Demean, Demean, Demean!

This will be hard for some of you. So, let me help you by giving you a few canned answers to put into play when Joe Creative gets one of his "outside the box" ideas.

### Option #1:

"Uh, Joe, now is not the time or place for creativity." This is a good first response. However, it does leave the door open for Joe to try again. It may squelch the idea but it won't squash Joe.

**Option #2:**

"Uh, Joe, that is the worst idea I've ever heard." This one has a little more heat: Advantage LOUDER.

**Option #3:**

Just stand up and walk out of the meeting. **BOOM!** That will get it done, I promise.

# 5
# END WITH THE BEGINNING IN MIND

— ✦✦✦ —

THE LEADERSHIP PRINCIPLE of "Begin with the End in Mind" has been pushed down our throats for years. Let's be honest, nobody really knows where this stuff is going to end up. I've never started a project that ended up like I thought it would.

The LOUDERSHIP principle of "Ending with the Beginning in Mind" is solid. Here is how it works.

Just get out there and get going. Ready—Fire—Aim! **BOOM!**

At some point you inevitably find your way to the end, good or bad. It doesn't really matter how you got there does it? It only matters that you are there. All you really need to do as a LOUDER is amplify the result, not the journey. It's the result that matters anyway—**BOOM!**

LOUDERS are product over process...results over relationships.

Here's a little bonus LOUDERSHIP principle. If you get to the end and the result is good, remind everyone with great veracity that you deserve the credit. It's good LOUDERSHIP. Trust me.

Now, if you get to the end and it wasn't good... put that bus in reverse...Joe Creative spoke up one too many times. It's time to squash him! Avoid the box that he was standing next to when he thought of that stupid idea. Remember, you just might need it later. **BOOM!**

The other benefit of Ending with the Beginning in Mind is that it is MUCH less work. I mean MUCH less work. Scratch all the lessons you learned in strategic planning, building consensus, and leading through change. None of that is needed when you "End with the Beginning in Mind." In fact, you can even cross out the need for communication. If nobody knows where they are heading, then your job becomes REALLY easy.

Now understand people who have no direction tend to do one of a couple of things.

First, they pack up and head somewhere that they can find more fulfillment and enjoyment in their work. Don't sweat that at all. Attrition is a natural part of organizational culture. In fact, in a LOUDER culture it is expected and even encouraged. Most leadership consultants will tell you that staff retention is a good thing and losing people all of the time is a sign of an unhealthy organizational culture.

Well, uh, they are WRONG—DEAD WRONG—INCREDIBLY WRONG!!! I don't really have a good argument on why they are wrong but I figured ALL CAPS and sounding emphatic would be enough. If I were teaching you this stuff in person, I would have also pounded my fist on the desk and then got up and walked out.

Leaving you confused is almost as valuable as leaving you convinced. **BOOM!**

# 6
# REINVENT THE WHEEL

———— ✦✦✦ ————

MOST LEADERS SAY there's no reason to "Reinvent the Wheel." Those leaders aren't ignorant; they just have too much wrong information.

The truth is, the wheel is likely one of the greatest inventions of all time and no one—absolutely NO ONE—knows who invented it in the first place. So the first LOUDERSHIP principle to exercise is what I call CAPITALIZATION. The wheel or any other unclaimed success is a perfect opportunity to CAPITALIZE on someone else's ingenuity and talent. I'm not saying you'll get away with telling people you invented the wheel. What I am saying is that as the leader you are in a perfect position to capitalize on other people's successes.

Now this'll be hard, because you hired dull and you just backed that bus over Joe. So, you'll likely have to go outside camp to find these unique opportunities.

Let me give you a practical example. Let's say you are the pastor of a church. You guys have about 300 or so people coming on Sundays. Your team meetings are producing little results as your dullards are scared to death to say anything. So, where do you go for ideas? Go to some big mega-church and just borrow what they've spent so much time and energy putting together. Just do what they're doing…no questions asked. They invented the wheel—borrow it.

It's unlikely that this will work out like you think. Remember though, it doesn't matter. You will get to an end at some point. If it's a good end, then—**BOOM!**—take credit—CAPITALIZE.

If it's a bad end, well, you're in trouble because Joe is down and this wheel you borrowed is going to be in your hands. This is the great part of lacking innovation and initiative. You know that mega-church pastor that figured it all out. Blame it on that guy. Don't worry I go more fully into this LOUDERSHIP Principle in Chapter 6, titled, "It's Not Your Fault."

By the way, if you drove the bus well, you only ran over Joe and the box you think inside of is still intact. If you remember, I told you that you may need it at some point. In fact, it's just this kind of moment that inspired me to have you do a picture exercise of that box earlier in the book. Remember it, it's cozy…it's safe…it's comfortable.  So, take a snack with you and get on in there and chill. There will be many more days ahead where you can CAPITALIZE on other people's talent.

# 7
# IT'S NOT YOUR FAULT

—— ✦✦✦ ——

I'VE HEARD IT SAID that "Any time you point a finger, that you have three pointing back to you." While that is an anatomically correct statement, there are some SERIOUS problems with the logic because it does not consider the thumb—AT ALL.

I don't know if you've noticed, but the opposable thumb is pretty important to our species and MUST be considered when we score points to determine fault. Consider these facts: Without the thumb, we couldn't tie our shoes, open jars, catch a ride when our car breaks down or affirm people when we are in deep agreement.

Still don't believe me? Let me demonstrate the importance of the thumb right now.

IfIweretonotusemythumbswhiletypingthisbookall ofmywordswouldruntogetherbecauseIusemythumbs tohitthespacebar.

At this point, only a moron would not agree with me that the thumb is VITALLY important and MUST be factored into in the whole finger pointing equation.

Now for the LOUDERSHIP logic: HINT—I'm about to drop a serious **BOOM!**

To work this equation out properly, we must assign a point value to each finger. We've already come to agreement that the thumb is extra valuable. So, we will give it a value of 2. Let's give the pointing finger a value of 1.

Let's give the middle finger and ring finger each a value of 1 as well. Now that only leaves the pinky. Let's be honest with each other here. The pinky is one of the least important phalanges. It just is. It's smaller and weaker than the others and therefore we must give it a value of less than 1. So let's give the pinky ½ point.

To recap:

Thumb = 2
Pointing = 1
Middle = 1
Ring = 1
Pinky = ½

Now do me a favor and point at the book. Go ahead, just point. Don't point at it like you are holding a gun and about to shoot—just do a good ol' fashion point.

Notice something? You're pointing finger and your thumb are aligned, aren't they? If not, you don't know how to point and can't be a LOUDER.

So what's the score now? Yep, it's 3 − 2.5. Do the math—It's NOT Your Fault!

# 8
# IF AT FIRST YOU DON'T SUCCEED—TRY SOMETHING ELSE

———— ✦✦✦ ————

SERIOUSLY THE IDEA of "Try, Try, Again" is an over-rated principle espoused by leaders for generations. I have NO idea where it came from but it's time to BLOW IT UP.

The LOUDERSHIP principle is the 21$^{st}$ Century approach: "If at first you don't succeed, TRY SOMETHING ELSE." **BOOM!**

Yep, you heard me. Try something else. Give up. Just quit. People who say, "I've never quit anything" are just downright stubborn. Stubbornness is not an endearing quality. For too long, these overachievers have blown the curve for the rest of us. It is high time we run those folks out of leadership and install a new order—the "Order of the Ordinary" as I like to call it.

Some people will challenge me on this LOUDERSHIP principle. I take that challenge. They might say that real leaders know how to press through. They will say that real leaders are resilient. They will say that real leaders never give up on their dreams. They will say that real leaders will see it through to the end. They will probably even try to tell you about Henry Ford's bankruptcy or how Abraham Lincoln lost several smaller elections before becoming the first President of the United States.

Those are inadequate arguments. Not because they aren't founded in some truth, but mainly because I don't agree with their position.

Let's think with LOUDERSHIP logic. If you continue to "Try, Try Again," what are you really doing? You're wasting time. You could have spent all of your "Try, Try Again" time on a new idea. That's why I say, "If at first you don't succeed, TRY SOMETHING ELSE." Seriously, just quit. Move on. Time is money.

I do need to point out the flashing yellow light in this principle. There will be people who

question your character because they just don't get
LOUDERSHIP. Don't worry. I know how to combat
this type of attack. Trust me, I've jumped ship more
than most and have come away virtually unscathed.

Here is how you do it—LOUDLY and I mean
LOUDLY—with great emphasis—proclaim that
there is a NEW VISION. Seriously, this will work
every time—especially if you just jump right in
to this new vision full force. Oh and don't worry
about not having a vision. This is LOUDERSHIP.
Remember, we end with the beginning in mind.

So just jump right in to the deep end of the
vision pool. I'm talking cannonball—big splash.
Just dive right in. Swim around a minute and make
a lot of hand movements. I'm telling you it works
EVERY time. Well, at least once or twice. Don't
forget though—attrition is natural. You can pull a re-
run on this in Q4 when your staff turns over.

# 9
# IF NO ONE IS FOLLOWING

———— ✦✦✦ ————

TELL ME IF YOU'VE HEARD this one question before: "If you turn around as a leader and no one is following, are you really a leader?"

At first blush, I guess I understand where they're coming from on this one. You would never guess how many times as a leader, I've turned around and didn't see a soul following me. It's like there is tumbleweed rolling around. I can't see anyone for miles.

If you look at the question a little more deeply, there is a rather insulting implication that the responsibility falls on the leader to make sure people are following. That may be the case for leaders — but not for LOUDERS. This scenario creates absolutely no introspection in me at all. We all know that the real issue is that the people behind you are just SLOW. **BOOM!**

I know, it's a harsh reality. But if we aren't honest with others, how can we be honest with ourselves. I speak more about the issue of honesty and integrity in an upcoming chapter. But for now, it's suffice to say that honesty, at least in the situations where we are being honest with others in an effort to get them to move along, is critical. There may be other situations, where it is not as critical. But in this situation it is vitally important. You may think this isn't a sound approach but it's built on sound principles of situational ethics.

The truth is that it's hard for others to keep up with us, especially if they are stuck in "Try, Try Again" mode. You and I are on to something else. We are pioneers, thought leaders, trend setters. It's not even fair for us to think that the people following will keep pace.

I am going to be very vulnerable with you, because by now, I know you know my heart for people. While I abound in compassion, I must say that this is one of the most frustrating things about LOUDERSHIP to me.

Sometimes I just want to turn around and yell, "PICK UP THE PACE." But my heart goes out to them. So, I know it's not the best approach, but the only way I've figured out how to overcome this after 20 years of LOUDERSHIP is simply **<u>don't turn around</u>**.

# 10
# UNTEGRITY

I KNOW YOU ARE THINKING that I just made a typo. But I didn't. I won't say I never make mistakes but they are rare. I think the last time I mad a typo was in 1998.

I specifically took the "I" out of Integrity and put in a "U." Strong leaders talk all the time about integrity. If you ask me, it's a little bit self-centered. It evens starts with the letter "I." The LOUDER focuses on the U, not the I. See what I did there? I just made one little vowel movement and centered the attention on U. **BOOM!**

The best part of this LOUDERSHIP principle called Untegrity is that it demands integrity from U (others) and it takes I (the louder) out of the equation. In other words, the I is no longer bound. The I is released from integrity, opening up all kinds of options on how to deal with situations.

I know this sounds dangerous but it's not. It's a numbers game. Let's say there are 10 people on staff, including you. If there are enough other people (let's say 9 out of 10) that are scrupulous and above reproach, that means that as a whole your business is at 90% integrity. Uh, that's hall of fame numbers if you ask me.

Let me give you a practical example of how releasing the "I" from Integrity can work out for you.

I was doing some one-on-one coaching with a LOUDER of a non-profit Christian ministry. This ministry was offered a $500,000 donation (which equals ½ the size of their budget). The only catch was that the money came with a "stipulation." To accept the donation, the ministry would have to make a slight change in their doctrinal statement. I can't remember the exact wording, but it didn't seem like that big of a deal to me. He was worried about taking "tainted" money. I told him that "the only thing wrong with tainted money is that there TAINT enough of it."

UNTEGRITY—**BOOM!**

# 11
## ORGANIZATIONAL
## CULTURE

CREATING A POSITIVE CULTURE in your organization is very important. This is one point that I agree with the leaders on. I mean, the last thing you as a LOUDER wants floating around the office is a bad vibe.

I know what you're thinking. You're recalling that I spoke out against creating a healthy organizational culture in a previous chapter. Well, you'd be right. But there is some madness to my method, I promise. I have a few very solid reasons I am waffling. First, I changed my mind. I have the right to do that. Secondly, I am modeling a LOUDERSHIP principle I call "The 180 Degree Louder." I know, it's artful the way I weave this stuff throughout the narrative. I told you I was brilliant.... **BOOM**!

Oh, and don't worry, I'm planning on flip-flopping back to my deep convictions about office culture in Chapter 17, which is titled "Morale or Lessrale."

While I agree with the leaders on this...there is more than one way to skin a cat. So, while I say yes to positive culture. I say NO to the age old, time consuming approach of building rapport, engaging people in leadership, creating ownership and all that bull. Seriously, that takes too much time and effort. And with the turnover that occurs in my business, I can't even think about a long lasting approach to development.

The LOUDER way is much simpler. Use the "Three (3) Step Process" I detail below and I will guarantee a positive organizational culture.

**Step #1:**

Surround yourself with YES men! **BOOM!**

What creates a more negative environment around your office than people challenging your ideas and leadership? Nothing, I say, NOTHING!

This won't be hard. In fact, due to my sound teaching regarding who you hire, it's likely already a given that you've hired yes men and women. In other words, when you "hired dull" you've already surrounded yourselves with folks that won't challenge you or your LOUDERSHIP. So, great job! You're catching on!!!

**Step #2:**

Doughnuts.

Not every morning, that's a budget drain. I'm talking once a quarter, TOPS! Oh, and don't worry about the expensive, local bakery kind. Just roll by the grocery and pick up a box of white powder doughnut holes. Set them out on the table. Talk about a boost in positivity...doughnuts...**BOOM**... works every time.

I promise you if you come by my office on doughnut day all you will see is smiles and little white powder fingerprints on the keyboards.

Now you may be thinking that even the doughnut thing is a bit over the top. I smell what you're stepping in, my LOUDER friend.

**Step #3:**

I got nothing.

# 12
## MAJOR ON THE MINORS

OKAY, I'M GOING TO BE HONEST. This LOUDERSHIP principle is going to be a tough one to convince you of so I'm not really going to try very hard. I'm just going to ask you to trust me on this one.

For so long, you've been taught that as a leader we have to "Put the big rocks in first," or "That the main thing is to keep the main thing the main thing." It has been ingrained into our heads that micro-management is bad and that those of us at the top of the chart need to be looking at the "big picture."

I can't tell you why I think this, maybe it's just a LOUDERSHIP hunch. But I think this whole "macro-level" stuff is just a fad. Micro-management is making a comeback. **BOOM!** We've seen this kind of thing happen before (think Bell Bottoms and

Leg Warmers). It's just how the world works. We go through cycles.

The question you have to ask yourself is this: Do you want to be the one holding on to the old way of doing things when the tide does turn? Or do you want to be on the front edge of the micro-management wave when it hits?

Let me remind you that LOUDERS are risk takers.

Some of you need some help on this one...so although it is time consuming, I will oblige. Here are some ways to get ahead of the curve and get back to micro-management.

- Screen everything. Nothing can go out of my office without my approval.

- Time cards. It's time to bring back the "clock" and require it to be punched.

- Daily work agendas must be submitted to the LOUDER by 8:30 a.m.

- Daily reports for work must be submitted to me by the close of your shift—7 p.m.

- Attend and lead all meetings, no matter what!

- Occasionally, just stand over someone's shoulder while they work. Don't say anything, just loom. **<u>BOOM</u>!**

# 13
# OVER PROMISE, UNDER DELIVER

———— ✦✦✦ ————

YOU'VE HEARD IT SAID, "Under Promise, Over Deliver."
Not bad…Not bad. But peep this LOUDERSHIP
principle: "Over Promise, Under Deliver!" **BOOM-
BOOM! DOUBLE BOOM!**

Yeah, that's right, I did it. I flipped the script.
See, I took the words and rearranged them in such
a way that the focus is now on the promise, not
the delivery. This is Sales 101. As a LOUDER the
promise is everything, EVERYTHING. It's the
point of sale if you will. If you don't make the right
promise, you won't get the sale. And you absolutely,
100% can't deliver if you don't get the sale. It's like
the old golf adage: 100% of putts that don't get to
the cup, don't go in the hole.

So what's more important: Promise or Delivery?
That's right, PROMISE. Here are four tips on how
to make a promise.

**Tip #1:**

Language is CRITICAL. Use phrases like "Trust me" or "Let me be totally honest."

Face it, nothing breeds trust like someone saying "trust me" a bunch of times. I said it in the introduction, remember? I said, "Trust me, I'm brilliant." This little phrase gives people security. It lets them know up front that you recognize that they think you might be coming off a little untrustworthy. So, just repeat, "Trust me" a few times. It will ease their minds…setting you up to make that sale.

**Tip #2:**

Language is CRITICAL. Yes, I know I said that already. I am doing it for emphasis and to highlight the real tip here which is what I call "Repetitive Redundancy."

Repetitive redundancy is a beautiful tool to use when overpromising and under delivering. Pick a phrase and then just use it over and over. Something big and catchy. Something with oompf. Like **BOOM!**

Then just stick it into your pitch over and over again. It will build excitement. **BOOM!** If you can get people focused on this catch phrase then you

have won the battle. You won't have to deliver
on the promises because the only thing they will
remember from your meeting is that you kept saying
**BOOM!**

This will release you from actually having to
deliver meaningful content. **BOOM!** For example,
if you were writing a book and your chapter looked
thin because you were out of ideas, you could insert
this catch phrase over and over again in an effort
to lengthen the chapter without actually saying
anything worthwhile. **BOOM!**

# 14
# FAIR TO MIDLIN'

MOST OF US HAVE BEEN TAUGHT leadership principles that will help us move from "Good to Great." You know the one that talks about the right people on the bus, in the right seats. I'm gonna blow this one up in 10, 9, 8, 7, 6, 5, 4, 3—**BOOM**—LOUDERSHIP principle—"Fair to Midlin!"

Why couldn't I let the countdown get all the way to zero? Because this LOUDERSHIP principle isn't for LOUDERS, it's for the people under us. Isn't that our job as LOUDERS?

You and I drive the bus. The wheel is firmly in my grip as the LOUDER. It's the people in the backity-back that need to move from good to great. You and I are already great. We were kind of born that way. That's why we drive the bus. I don't know how the "leaders" miss this fact.

Before I move on, let me get as "touchy-feely" as a LOUDER gets. You and I both know that there is a heaviness that comes with greatness that not all people can handle. To walk around, constantly knowing you are better than everyone else is a tough load to carry. It's pretty hard to have this knowledge and walk in humility like we do. But keep in mind; this is about others, not about us.

Now back to the "Fair to Midlin" principle. If you start great, like we did, you can't really help but be great. But aspiring to be great is pretty egotistical if you ask me so we don't want to encourage people to move toward greatness. Greatness should really be reserved for those of us who were born with it.

Let's be honest. Most people are not great. They're not even good. They are fair, average. I know it's a harsh reality but we are here to help them move from "Fair to Midlin'." That's what LOUDERS do. But I'm not going to look someone in the face and tell them that they are good and can become great if they are not and they won't. That's LIEDership. I don't do LIEDership.

I know it will be a harsh realization for them. But they have to look reality in the face sometimes before you can move forward. They may not ever thank you for adjusting the rear view mirror of the bus you're driving to the "honesty" setting but by coming to grips with this truth, they will be better and your organization will be better.

The best part of this principle is what it does for you as the LOUDER. Isn't that always the case? When we help others, it ultimately helps us. It's certainly not our motivation, but practicing LOUDERSHIP principles is always wIn, wIn.

The result that'll happen for you is that you'll continue to drive the bus. Let me explain:

If you can move your team to the reality that they are fair and the best they'll ever do is midlin', then you will create a culture of inadequacy. While this sounds like a negative, it's not. What occurs in a culture of inadequacy is people project the reality that they are "fair" onto everyone else. This is a good thing for two reasons. First, people don't get their hopes up. If you can create a culture of hopelessness, I can promise you that the most important seat on the bus will be yours forever.

# 15
# HUFFS,
# THE LONG STARE,
# AND THE POUNDING
# OF THE FIST

✦✦✦

I'M A SOFTY AT HEART, that's obvious. On occasion though, a LOUDER has to lay down the law if you know what I mean. I've developed quite a few LOUDERSHIP strategies over the years that are to be used when you have to discipline a team member. I've listed 5-7 particular strategies below.

Actually, I don't know how many will be listed below. I haven't written them yet and have no intention of editing or re-reading this book before it goes to print. Remember LOUDERS "End with the Beginning in Mind."

Anyway, these strategies are profoundly impactful and incredibly easy. They work best when you're in a group setting and you single out one person. In fact, I use all of these principles in that fashion. I never bring people in for one on one disciplinary action. It's practical really. If I can put someone in their place in front of the others, then I will strongly discourage any other person from the same maleficence. Did I spell that correctly? Don't care! **BOOM!**

**Strategy #1:**

*The Exaggerated Huff*—I love a short, simple huff. It is a breathy gesture that expresses displeasure. This little gem can be used in all kinds of situations. You can huff when someone says something stupid or when they come up with an idea that you dislike. But the principle I am teaching here, The EXAGGERATED HUFF is more advanced. The exaggerated huff is the simple huff on steroids.

There are three primary concepts to master in the exaggerated huff. First, you must develop a STRONG, and I mean STRONG eye roll to go along with the huff. Secondly, and as importantly, you must start the huff with a really hard PF at the beginning. Don't worry, you can't overdo this part. Thirdly, and most importantly is the length of the huff. The exaggerated huff has to last at LEAST three seconds.

Try it with me right now....say it...pffff.

That was pitiful. Try it again, with conviction. And stress the PPPPFFFFFFFF.

Now hold it....HOLD it....HOLD IT—**BOOM!**

**Strategy #2:**

*The Long Stare*—Yep, it's that simple really. Don't move a muscle. Just stare intently...REALLY intently for at least 2 minutes. Two minutes is a LONG time for silence. Don't break eye contact. Peer into their eyes...it's a quiet assassination. At the end of two minutes, precisely, raise your eyebrows ever so slightly and ever so slowly (practice it right now) and then say in a very low voice, "You understand me now right." **BOOM!**

**Strategy #3:**

*Socrates 'em*—This approach is a combination of the Socratic method of asking questions and a middle school argument. The best thing is that there is NO thought required on this one —NONE! All you have to do is repeat what they are saying in a question form. This is like waterboarding it's so annoying. Here's an example:

Employee: "Sir, I laid a copy of the annual budget on your desk."

LOUDER: "Oh, so you LAID a copy of the annual budget on my desk, huh?"

Employee: "Yes, I put it right next to your phone on your desk."

LOUDER: "Really, you put it RIGHT next to the PHONE on my desk?"

See how that could really get under someone's skin? Advantage—LOUDER! **BOOM!**

**Strategy #4:**

*One Minute Angrier*—I know we've all been taught the one minute manager. I prefer the "One Minute Angrier." This one is for the advanced LOUDERS among you because it is incredibly hard to pull off. The concept is to throw the biggest temper fit/tirade possible in 60 seconds. The "one minute" is crucial to this approach and the reason it is SO difficult. Sure, all LOUDERS can throw a fit, but how many of us can do it in ONE minute and have the discipline to end it abruptly? Everyone has heard your unending rants. The one minute angrier is full out, crazy person for one minute, then the slam of a door on your way out. (Oh, and test the door. A slow closing door KILLS this strategy).

**Strategy #5:**

*Pound the Table*—This approach is one I mentioned earlier in the book. Only put this one in play after you've tried the others. It's HEAVY! It's a very simple move—just pound the table with your fist. You can ramp it up a bit if you throw in lots of hand gestures and body twitches before you commit to the pound. If it's a really tough case, you can always do it with a long stare and the exaggerated huff.

Works nearly EVERY time—**BOOM!**

# 16
# B.T.A.G.'s

YOU'VE ALL HEARD of BHAG's right?

Big—Hairy—Audacious—Goals. The principle being taught by leaders through this catchy little acrostic (might be an acronym, I don't really know the difference) is pretty simple. We are being taught to set forth goals that are big. We are taught to set goals that inspire people. In other words, dream BIG. We are taught to set goals that take a whole team to accomplish them.

Quite honestly, that kind of thinking is less than average.

The LOUDERSHIP version of this principle is superior in every way. LOUDERS don't set BHAG's we set BTAGs

Benign—Tepid—Ambiguous—Goals

Tick, Tick, Tick, Tick, Tick, Tick ---- **BOOM!**

Oops, I did it again… I BLOWED IT UP!!!

BTAG's are the goals you want to set, I promise. The logic is simple but profound. A big, hairy, audacious goal is hard to accomplish. We want people to succeed, especially ourselves, right? If that is the case, why in the world would we set out to do something that we might fail trying? Leaders always talk about "failing forward." LOUDERS say don't risk failure. Failure hurts badly, so I've heard.

The only surefire way to not fail is to set a goal that you are either assured of reaching (a benign, tepid goal) or one that is so ambiguous that no one will really know if you accomplished it or not.

Setting benign, tepid goals is the easy part. Making them ambiguous is tough, but I will get to that in a minute, maybe.

Here are some hints on how to do benign and tepid:

- Don't use action verbs, especially power verbs.

- Use flowery language, soften it up a bit.

- Start your goals with the words, "That, the."

- Use a lot of words.

- Use a double negative if necessary.

The art of ambiguity is a little more difficult to pull off, but that's okay, because you're a LOUDER. The reason it's difficult is because you have undoubtedly learned about setting S.M.A.R.T. objectives at the last 9 leadership conferences you have attended. Don't worry, I'm about to come through, as I always do.

So, here are some tips to keep things ambiguous:

- Don't, under any circumstances, assign a timeline to the goal.

- Resist the need to use measurements of any kinds, especially numbers.

- Assign multiple team members to the goal without appointing any specific staff.

- Don't write them down. I promise, writing down goals will bite you one day.

- Don't bring them up at staff meetings. In fact, just refrain from mentioning them at all.

BTAG's—**BOOM!!**—That's LOUDERSHIP!

# 17
# MORALE
# OR LESSRALE

⸺ ✦✦✦ ⸺

SOME WILL TRY TO TELL YOU that a happy workplace is a productive workplace. Uh, they're lying. It's not true. I don't know why they've chosen to lie. Maybe they're just bad people and don't like being honest. I'm not sure. Nonetheless, they're lying and I for one am not buying what they're selling.

I'm 42 years old and I've been a LOUDER for 42 of those years. And if one thing is a certainty it's that a happy workplace is a less productive workplace. It's a simple LOUDER logic.

Time is money. Happiness wastes time.

Let me explain. If your employees are yucking it up at the office cooler, they're WASTING TIME. If they're going out to lunch together because they enjoy each other's company and are friends, you mark my words; they will turn the 18 minute lunch break into 25, WASTING TIME. If everyone is walking around, "Hi Bobbing" each other, in other words looking up from their work and saying "Hi Bob" when a co-worker walks by, well they're WASTING TIME.

Remember, quarterly donuts are all you need to create the organizational culture you're looking for. It's not your job to create a "happy place" where everyone is "enjoying their work" or "feeling valued." It's your job to get things done, baby. The way I do that as a LOUDER is by ensuring that every moment of every day is productive. My mind is on the money and the money's on my mind. I am profit and production over people, every day, ALL DAY.

So, as a LOUDER I don't want MORale—I want LESSrale. **BOOM!** Heads down people—get back to work!

Now reversing this trend won't be easy. Your employees have likely worked under a leader with a total lack of insight on this issue. So, they may come into your company and have the unrealistic expectation that you guys are about staff morale. Don't worry though. The tips I am about to share with you will get you building LESSrale really quickly. You can do it!

**Tip #1:**

*Chain of Commode*—Read that one again. Yep, chain of commode. One of the biggest time wasters at your office is the bathroom. So, I lock the bathroom and make people <u>check out the key from me</u> when they need to go potty. This will cut down on the bathroom trips. Especially if you put the key on a big obtrusive object, like they do at the gas station. Think tire rim or cinder block but use something from the office, like maybe a paper cutter.

**Tip #2:**

*Ice Cubicles*—Every once in a while, turn the A/C unit down, WAY down. I know it is counterintuitive because you think the energy cost will go up. You're right. However, the productivity from your employees goes WAY up when they are freezing cold. It just makes sense because people will need to work hard to stay warm. LOUDER LOGIC!

**Tip #3:**

*Speed Lunch*—Institute the 18 minute lunch break that I mentioned earlier. People don't need more than 18 minutes, I promise. It's a proven fact that I have noticed without research that people are eating faster today than they ever have before. Capitalize on this trend and you can really increase productivity.

FYI – speed lunches don't apply to us—just the team. Remember, your box is on top. Let it be known that you've earned the long lunch. Take your time. Run some errands and eat up. A heavy meal will help around 3:00 p.m. when you need a short nap in your office.

**Tip #4:**

***Pay to Play***—Another time waster in the office is playtime on the computer. It used to be solitaire that ate away at productivity. Now it is Youtube and Facebook. Some would say that a funny Youtube clip floating around your office keeps things light, makes it an enjoyable place to be. I say Youtube, Facebook and any other activity that moves people away from the work is WASTING TIME.

So, I decided to institute a policy in my office that fixes this issue and increases revenue. Ready? It's simple. Make employees pay for their internet service. In other words: "WIFI ain't free round here no mo'." I promise taking away free access to the internet will build LESSrale and in turn increase productivity.

The added bonus to this tip is that you are making MONEY and increasing profit. Do the math. If you have 10 employees paying $5.00 per day for internet service it adds up to $14,318 per year (give or take). That's MONEY in your pocket.

**Tip #5:**

***Benefits Come in Small Packages***—I'm not going to belabor this point. Everybody touts benefits and benefit packages. Well, here's a novel idea. You have one benefit as an employee here at LOUDER, Inc. And it is....drumroll please.....a paycheck. You have a job. Lots of people don't. Put your head down and get back to work.

# 18
# K.I.S.F.S.

THE KISS (KEEP IT SIMPLE STUPID) principle has been around for years...but I'm about to BLOW IT UP. Let me tell you why.

First, there is an inference here that I am stupid. Uh, I'm not stupid. I've got 27 credit hours toward my undergraduate degree that tell me so. Okay, 21, but I am still contesting the two leadership classes I failed. Can you believe that they expected me to attend classes that I should have been teaching?

My IQ and EQ are off the charts. NEVER would I call myself stupid like the KISS principle instructs and the inference is insulting.

The LOUDERSHIP principle is to "Keep it Simple for Stupids" or—K.I.S.F.S . **BOOM!!**

Let's be honest. If you are a LOUDER, in the midst of any group setting, you are the best and brightest. I've never looked around the table of people I employ and thought, "Man, these people are really smart."

As a LOUDER, I keep it simple for stupids.

For example, I utilize this LOUDERSHIP principle in this book. That's not for my benefit, but yours.

# 19
# NAMEDROPS KEEP FALLING ON MY HEAD

✦✦✦

WE ALL AGREE THAT NETWORKING is very important. In fact, I contend that network = net worth. So the next principle I'm going to teach you might in fact be the best money maker in this book. Watch me BLOW UP a leadership principle.

Leaders say, "It's not what you know but who you know."

LOUDERS say, "It's not who you know, it's who you pretend to know."

Ba-Ba-Ba————**BOOM!**

All LOUDERS must develop the art of dropping names. I've perfected this craft and promise I can convince you that I know anybody. Here's a scenario to teach you this principle.

Let's say you're in a conversation with a potential business partner and he says, "Do you know Jimmy Blankenship?"

Now you don't know Jimmy Blankenship from Adam. In fact, you can't think of one Jimmy you do know except your nephew, and he's 7. But before you blow this opportunity, let me give you some steps to success.

**Step #1:**

Say, "Jimmy Blankenship...yeah I know Jimmy." Remember to pause between the name of the person and...your affirmative answer. This gives you some wiggle room. You might need it momentarily.

**Step #2:**

Then say, "Jimmy Blankenship...he has dark hair right?" I know that seems like a risk but it's not. 75% of the world's hair color is dark. If you get a yes, then it's likely over right there. You have convinced this joker that you know Jimmy B.

### Step #3:

If Jimmer doesn't have dark hair, then say: "Oh
yeah, Jimbo. He's got blue eyes, right?" I know that
seems like a risk as well, but don't sweat it. If he
has blond hair, then the blue eye guess is going to
be right 9 out of 10 times. So, it's likely that by now
this potential partner is convinced.

### Step #4:

At this point, if you are way off, the guy across
from you will laugh and tell you either JB is bald
or has red hair. Don't worry! You can get out of this
with calling Jimmy a name a derogatory name. Say,
"Oh that Jimmy…that Jakeleg!"

**BOOM!**

# 20
# 1 HABIT OF A HIGHLY EFFECTIVE LOUDER

———— ✦✦✦ ————

I'VE HEARD SO MANY PEOPLE say that one of the most transformative books of their lives is the *7 Habits of Highly Effective People*. I have to be honest, sometimes. I liked it…but it was a little much. I mean 7 Habits? That's a lot of habits. What if I could simplify it? What if I could narrow down the 7 or the 11 or the 21 habits, laws and axioms down to just ONE?

Well, I can. And I will. **BOOM!**

The one Habit of a Highly Effective LOUDER is very simple: Be Skeptical.

I'm not saying you shouldn't trust anyone. I am saying you shouldn't trust everyone. Seriously, people are out to get you. Keep your eyes up and your ears to the ground. Everyone wants to be you. Jealousy abounds in and around you. Remember, it's

not your fault. You were born this way and you have
the IT factor.

Just to help you out, I'm going to list some
"guys" that you should really be skeptical of around
the office.

- Quiet, reflective guy

- No socks on with loafers guy

- Never forgets a birthday guy

- Wants to buy you lunch guy

- Car always super clean guy

- Short sleeve button up guy

Now, I recognize that much of my language is
about "guys" and about "men." I'd be the last person
on earth to be chauvinistic, obviously. Nonetheless,
I said hire "Yes Men" earlier and here I am talking
about the "guys" to be skeptical of in the office.

So I decided to also make a list of which women
you should be skeptical of in the office. However,
the only one I could come up with was "cat lady."
You know, the woman who has a cat key chain. Her
ring tone says, "MEOOOOW." You know her, the
one who has framed pictures of her cats on the desk?

Come on seriously, cat lady, the one who ALWAYS wears the airbrushed cat T-Shirt with a pic of Tubby for casual Friday. I know you know her, keep acting like you don't…big chicken.

# 21
# THINK LONG,
# THINK WRONG

MOST LEADERS WILL TELL YOU that making tough
decisions is one of the main parts of leadership.
They're right, but not because they're smart. I mean,
that's kind of a no brainer, right?

What they're wrong about is how to go about
making the tough decisions. They use stuff like
data assimilation, management teams, think tanks,
advisory boards, and focus groups. Some have
whole departments dedicated to R & D. By the time
a decision gets made with these types of leaders, the
opportunity has likely passed.

LOUDERS are different. We don't need all
that crap and we don't tarry on decision making.
**BOOM!**

We are quick thinkers. You know what to
do in your gut...so do it...no worries. And don't

sweat it if you make a bad decision. By this point, you should be a spin doctor…you should be able to work your way out of it or just hide in the box. But if you're not there yet, you're probably used to catching things more slowly than most. And I'm used to people like you. So, Chapter 22 is a step-by-step guide to the art of reversing course.

Here are some bullets on how to make quick decisions:

- Go with your gut. Every time. No questions asked.

- Don't sleep on it. You know what to do now. Do it.

- Don't seek counsel. They don't have a clue nor do they have to execute the decision.

- Data is lame. In fact, data has never made a decision in its life. And if the people around you ask about data, give them a really hard to understand chart that is printed in grayscale. That way, you can manipulate it to say whatever you want.

Remember (and let everyone else know) that the decision is yours and yours alone. And then move forward, fast and furious. Don't look back. Get to 100 mph as fast as possible.

# 22
# THE 180° LOUDER

SOME OF YOU (the slow ones) are thinking: "What if I make the wrong decision?" "What if it backfires?" Never fear…LOUDERSHIP is here.

There's a lot of teaching out there about the 360 Degree Leader. I'm not sure what that means exactly. Maybe it teaches you how to be well rounded. Again, I'm insulted. Remember, you and I were born with this IT thing. We are well rounded. There's no need for introspection or review. What's done is done. And we're done.

The principle I want to teach here is the 180 Degree LOUDER or the Art of Reversing Course.

Say that decision you made quickly, without much thought or analysis comes back to bite you in the butt. Odds are that it won't. You were likely right on the money. But in the minute chance that your gut was off a little bit because of that burrito you ate for lunch, well you have to figure out how to get out of that decision. That's what I like to call the art of reversing course.

Here's a step-by-step plan on how to reverse course.

**Step #1:**

### *Remember Chapter 7*—It's Not Your Fault!

You remember Chapter 7 don't you? If not, point your finger at the book demonstratively and I promise it will come back to you. In fact, you will likely never point again without doing some basic math. That's a free gift with the book. You're welcome!

Bottom line…It's <u>not</u> your fault! Start pointing vigorously at the people around you. If you look around and don't see anyone, just blame everyone. Something will stick.

**Step #2:**

### *Find a scapegoat*—This one won't be easy because you told everyone that it was your decision. But it can be done. I usually pick someone from IT or Accounting. There isn't really any good reason to pick someone from one of those departments. It just feels right to me.

**Step #3:**

*Apologize!*—Wait a second…not for yourself. It's NOT YOUR FAULT!! Apologize for the mistakes of your team that led you to make the decision. Make sure you hear me clearly. You aren't apologizing for anything you did or even a wrong decision. You're humbly requesting that the whole company or organization find it in their heart to forgive the people that informed you incorrectly. It's brilliant really. It communicates that not only was this decision not your fault but that you are a compassionate LOUDER, hoping to assuage any negative feelings toward the people who failed the company.

**BOOM**—180 degrees.

# 23
# THE EMAIL ADVANTAGE

EMAIL IS PROBABLY one of the greatest inventions of the 19<sup>th</sup> century. If it's used properly, it can be of GREAT benefit to you as a LOUDER. I know you're not stupid. You likely have the competency to turn on a computer, check your inbox, and correspond via the World Wide Web.

However, there are some nuances to this email stuff that you should know as a LOUDER that no one out there is teaching. Don't worry though, I'm here for you, bro.

First thing first though…I need to explain the macro concept I'm teaching here before I get into the details.

With that said, let me now detail the specifics of how to use email to your advantage!

a.) Urgent button—I don't know if you've seen this little button on your email but it is very important that you find it and click it before you send every email. The urgent button puts a little red flag next your email when someone sees it in their inbox. This signifies that what you have to say is of utmost importance…which shouldn't have to be stated…but remember who you're working with here.

b.) CAPS are AWESOME, especially in email— You've seen me use them through this book. Again, they bring attention to important stuff.

c.) Grammar and Punctuation are important: see point B to better understand my point here; commas and hyphens make things read more easily.

d.) Extra-long responses from you are good. Use email not only to talk through quick issues, but use it to convey philosophical principles.

e.) Emails are also great to use for confrontational issues. Because words in an email don't convey emotion or the inflection of my voice, they can often be misunderstood. Some people say that it bad. I say it's good because it keeps people guessing and confused. Remember leaving people confused is as good as leaving them convinced.

f.) Don't even try to respond to every email. You're the LOUDER. You choose what you want to respond to and don't want to respond to. If you don't have time or don't want to, just hit delete and move on. Don't keep it in your email box either. It's a downer for you to keep seeing it in there. It makes you feel like you're not doing your job, which isn't correct. If you choose not to respond, you've done your job.

g.) Learn this line: "I've been having server problems."

I know these are simple and you've likely used them already but if you can employ them more consistently, I promise you will gain an advantage on those you lead. And isn't that the point?

**BOOM!**

# 24
# THE ART OF MEETING

THERE IS NO SCIENCE to running good meetings…
it's an art…and I am Rembrandt. For you to be a
LOUDER, you have GOT to, I mean GOT to be able
to perfect the ART of meeting for extended periods
of time without accomplishing anything. So, forget
about agendas, reports and action items like all the
leadership gurus teach.

They're worthless! Not the gurus…just their
concepts.

They're outdated! Not the concepts…just the
gurus.

Anyway, follow the LOUDER. I won't lead you
anywhere, much less astray.

**Principle #1:**

*Give me 10*—Right when the meeting is about
to start, walk through the conference room on your

cell phone (you don't actually have to be on a call)
and mouth these words while pointing at your watch:
"Give me 10."

That sets a tone. The tone is that what you are
doing…and in fact you…are worth waiting for.

**Principle #2:**

*Scrap the agenda!*—It's wrong and terribly
insensitive for you to go into a meeting with an
agenda.  Everyone will see straight through you.
Remember, it's about the people…like I've said
through this whole book.

Just wing it. We're in a post-modern society. You
know what that means, right?

**Principle #3***:*

*Notes are for chumps!*—LOUDERS don't need
a notepad. It makes you look weak.

**Principle #4:**

*Take the Call!*—Some people say it's
unprofessional to use your cell phone in a meeting.
Uh, they're wrong. It actually shows the people you're
meeting with how busy you are and how important you
are. That's a good thing. It indicates to them that the

importance of what you're discussing in the meeting doesn't rank with the important things you have to do as a LOUDER. Another good thing.

**Principle #5:**

*Interrupt*—There's no sense listening to people if what they say is stupid or uninformed. It wastes time. And time is money. So, just go ahead and nip it in the bud. Interrupt them and move on.

If you're a good LOUDER, you'll know exactly how to do this principle. You should have already been using their "talk time" to formulate what you were going to say anyway because you always manage your time well.

**Principle #6:**

*Chase the rabbit*—He's cute...

**Principle #7:**

If you're still reading these, there's something wrong with you.

# 25
# THE LOUDERSHIP
# QUOTIENT–LQ

—— ✦✦✦ ——

THIS CHAPTER IS MEANT to be interactive–participatory.
I don't advise this strategy in LOUDERSHIP. It's
actually not good in most situations. However, it
seemed like the best approach for this particular
chapter.

So here we go…it's quiz time. I want you to
answer the following questions. The result of the end
of this chapter is that you'll get a clear picture of
your LOUDERSHIP quotient, or LQ. It's like an IQ
but more important. It's a way to let you see where
you stand and where you need to grow. This kind
of self evaluation is also that something that I don't
recommend doing often, but it fits.

So, here you go:

Gauge your responses with a simple yes or no.
At the end, I'll help you do the math.

1. Do you ever use your time wisely during conversations by formulating what you're about to say instead of listening to what someone else is saying?

2. Have you have ever told someone you were having lunch with that you would fire the server if you were in charge?

3. Do you ever look around the room and think of yourself better than everyone else?

4. Have you said "Amen" to any part of this book?

5. Do you ever yell through the wall instead of using the phone intercom?

6. Do you ever sneak up on your employees just to scare them?

7. Do you ever ask one of the "girls" in your office to make you some "mud" referring to a pot of coffee?

8. Do you ever use the word subordinate with your employees?

9. Do you ever look around and no one is following?

10. Do you wish others would just be more like you and do things right?

Okay, here's the math. Each affirmative answer to a question is worth 1 point. Let's see how you did.

Scale:

10—Cream of the Crop—right up there with me!

9—You're SOOOO close. Press on my friend.

8—You've got some work to do. Maybe consider a LOUDER coach. I'm not available.

7—It's like you're not even trying.

6—Embarrassing, really.

5—I don't have time for this, moving on.

# 26
# BECOMING
## ✦✦✦

IF YOU DIDN'T READ my second introduction, you may have missed my warning regarding satire. Hopefully, you figured that out quickly and don't think I'm really the LOUDER that I'm representing in the material.

A large percentage of the content that I've presented is just nonsensical, farcical stuff that my brain thinks up when I should be sleeping. The hope was that this would be a way to teach the principles of leadership that we're all trying to grasp and take hold of through a uniquely humorous approach.

There are portions of this book though, I shamefully admit, that come from a laundry list of mistakes that I've made over the past 20 years in leadership. I've lived out some of these LOUDERSHIP principles.

That pains me to say, but it's honest. And as I've presented these little chapters with business people in comedic form, I can tell that I'm not the only LOUDER in the room. In fact, several of the chapter titles actually came from friends offering up suggestions once they knew I was writing this book.

Truth be told, we've all done some of this stuff. Whether we recognize it or not, LOUDERSHIP has likely been at play in our leadership. Whether it was squashing a vision, blaming others, or withholding power, we've all done it.

I'm not sure what the root cause for this is for you but I can tell you that most of my leadership mistakes have come from my hubris. For almost half of my leadership career, I consistently thought more of myself (my intelligence, my ideas and my opinions) than others. I also consistently sought opportunity to advance myself and to hold power and control. Some of this was done subconsciously, I'm sure. But some of it was done with great intention.

Interestingly for me, my particular context is ministry leadership. That may seem odd to some reading, but just let me say that the LOUDER sickness abounds in church, ministry, family and business settings alike.

I still struggle with LOUDERHIP. But over the last eight years, I have been really blessed to be part of a community of leaders in Lexington that is helping me overcome myself. It's a family really. A family of really high quality, committed ministry leaders in Lexington, KY. We call ourselves Lexington Leadership Foundation (LLF). Our mission is to connect, unify and mobilize the Body of Christ so that Lexington will be transformed into a city for God.

The founder of our ministry, Dr. John Withers, has been the antidote to my personal LOUDERSHIP sickness. For some strange reason, he took a chance on me becoming his successor to this beautiful thing that God birthed in and through him. Each week since I was brought onto his team, I have been with him in what we call discipleship. It's really him using the Bible and his incredible life experiences to shape and mold me into a leader.

If those weekly lessons were all I received over the last eight years, it would likely be enough.

However, I've also been surrounded by men and women of incredible passion and great faith (the LLF Team). Quite honestly, my LOUDER tendencies don't really stand a chance in the midst of such greatness.

For example, there is no way for me to see myself (intelligence, ideas, or opinions) as superior when I am with this crew. In fact, I am greatly humbled to even be in the same room with them most days. Likewise, it would be futile for me to try to withhold power and authority where it has undoubtedly been bestowed in great measure with or without my approval.

This little micro unit of leaders is like family. Don't get me wrong, there have been incredibly rough moments in our history. Times that you have to release someone you love and care for deeply from employment is the toughest. Those instances have caused some incredibly sleepless nights.

Nonetheless, we are a community of people who love each other dearly. We aren't combative. We don't do rivalry. We believe the best in each other. We laugh together. We cry together. We watch Youtube clips together. We eat together. We sing together. We strategize together. We rejoice together. We mourn together. We share with each other and try to meet each other's needs when we have the ability. We pray together. We worship together.

It's such a joy.

You may be thinking: "Wow, the LOUDER has become a LEADER." It would be more correct to say, "WOW, the LOUDER is <u>becoming</u> a LEADER." And quite frankly, even those words can misplace credit.

The truth is that I am <u>becoming</u> a leader...but it's not because of a book I read or a conference I attended. Don't hear me incorrectly, I greatly respect the people that are positioned to move us forward as leaders. The barbs in the book were totally in jest. And, I truly am an advocate of reading the books and attending the conferences.

My <u>becoming</u> is really attributed to the rich, wonderful environment I find myself in every day of my life.

I figure I am going to be on the planet for another 40 years or so...continuing to become what God intended for me to be...a leader in His Kingdom. Leading my family. Leading my friends. Leading my city...all the while being led myself. And while I hope to still change the world (likely as you do), I graciously accept that it is me who is being changed.

I am grateful. Very grateful.

I hope you will pass my book onto others. If getting a glimpse of LOUDERSHIP, as ridiculous as it is, would advance someone's journey to <u>becoming</u> a better leader, I would be very happy.

Or, if a leader just gets a quick laugh out of it, that would be cool too.

# ACKNOWLEDGMENTS

There are so many people who shaped my leadership
and my heart. You know who you are and I won't be
able to capture it all here, yet I try.

*Kim Geary* — you're the one. Just to be able to look
into your eyes and hold your hand every day of my life
has been the most incredible gift God has ever given a
man. You are so beautiful and I can't imagine a day
on this planet without you. I am forever yours
and you are forever mine.

*Elijah Geary* — you are really incredible. The way
God has wired you just amazes. I love everything
about you, little man. You make me laugh and bring
me great joy. If I could pick any little boy on
the planet and call them my son, it would be you.
You're going to change the world!

*Pat Geary* — Mom, I am the man I am today because of you. Thank you for everything, including your sacrifice, your sense of humor, your dedication to me and my family, but mostly your unconditional love.

*Bob Geary* — "Artichokes, two for a dollar." "Hee-Haw, Hee-Haw, Hee-Hawlays calls me that!" You taught me how to tell a joke and tell a story. I'm proud to be your son.

*John Withers* — you taught me how to lead and allowed me to steward this great vision for our city. You've increased my faith and my freedom. I will never forget the moment you said, "Eric, don't take yourself so damn seriously."

*Bill Rouse* — dude, seriously. I've never had more fun with anyone in my life than with you. I can't imagine my life without you as my friend. Thank you.

*Steve Diggs* —your dedication and commitment to your calling are unsurpassed. Thanks for taking a chance on me in 1995.

*Rick Avare* — I've learned so much from you as a leader, a father, and a follower of The Way. Thank you for opportunities to live out my calling.


*Lexington Leadership Foundation Team* — I honestly can't wait to get to work every day just to be with all of you. You're amazing leaders, each of you. I love you all very much and am so thankful for the opportunity to lead.


*Marcus Patrick* — you've been with me now for my entire leadership career. If ever anyone has seen me live out the principles of this book it is you...sorry! Let's hug sometime.


*Tommy Green* — you're my best friend. Thank you.

# ABOUT THE AUTHOR

—◆◆◆—

ERIC GEARY LOVES JESUS. He is husband to Kim Geary and father to Elijah Geary. Eric serves as Chief Executive Officer of Lexington Leadership Foundation, a faith based non-profit agency in Lexington, KY.

Eric loves to have fun and make people laugh. The greatest compliment Eric has ever received is that "he can instantly move from the sublime to the ridiculous."

Eric is a great story teller and gifted communicator and he's never seen a microphone or a stage he didn't like. Eric welcomes comedic opportunities to teach the LOUDERSHIP principles at corporate events, leadership speaking engagements, workshops and seminars.

# LOUDERSHIP.COM

Visit loudership.com to:

- Read the LOUDERSHIP blog

- See video clips of Eric teaching LOUDERSHIP principles

- Book Eric for speaking engagements and corporate events

- Follow Eric on Twitter

- Order lots of books for your friends

# DEDICATION

To my wife Kim:

I love you with all of my heart. You make me laugh and smile.

To my son Elijah:

You're incredible.  Options are limitless. Chase your dreams. You have what it takes.

Follow Christ! Have fun!

CPSIA information can be obtained
at www.ICGtesting.com
Printed in the USA
FSHW021607100221
78468FS